Phonicability Games

VERA CONWAY

DIGRAPHS: EE OO AR OR SH CH TH AND CK

Phonicability Games

CONTENTS

INTRODUCTION 3

USING THIS BOOK 7

FIND THE BEGINNING ('CK' WORDS)........................ 8

FIND THE ENDING ('CK' WORDS) 12

GIVE THE DOG A BONE
(SINGLE-SYLLABLE 'CK' WORDS) 17

MISSING 'OO'S AND 'EE'S.................................... 25

THE 'OO' AND 'EE' MATCHING GAME 31

THE 'AR'/'OR' GAME 36

THE 'AR'/'OR' QUICKIE 43

THE 'SH'/'CH' GAMES 47

THE TONGUE-BETWEEN-YOUR-TEETH GAME............. 53

THE 'SH'/'CH'/'TH' GAME 56

Published by Hopscotch Educational Publishing Ltd,
29 Waterloo Place, Leamington Spa CV32 5LA
(Tel: 01926 744227)

© 2002 Hopscotch Educational Publishing

Written by Vera Conway
Series design by Blade Communications
Illustrated by Peter Dennis
Printed by Clintplan, Southam

ISBN 1-904307-16-7

Introduction

The idea of inventing games of this nature was first conceived out of sheer desperation when I met my first uncooperative pupil. He told me confidently, 'I do not need to learn to read because I am going to be an actor.' As he was then only seven years old and quite unable to project his mind into the future, no argument of mine could convince him to believe otherwise.

A year later when this boy was diagnosed as being severely dyslexic he was triumphant. He stubbornly closed his mind to everyone's attempts to help him, and his behaviour in school gave much cause for concern, but our lessons continued. I spent two hours with him each week and, in spite of himself, he learned to read and write. The almost-miracle was achieved by means of games we played together, which he actually enjoyed.

Since then, every game in this series has been played time and time again with pupils who have a variety of problems as well as with those who appear to learn to read and write without experiencing any difficulties. As I saw more and more pupils benefiting from playing the games, I wanted to share them with others – both old and young – so that they could experience the joy and laughter that come with learning to read and spell.

I hope, also, that school teachers, parent teachers and helpers of all kinds will become better acquainted with the simple logic of teaching reading and spelling by phonics (sounds).

This is by no means a return to something old-fashioned in a back-to-basics approach. We are all discovering the real worth of a teaching method which, speaking generally, has not been profoundly comprehended. Nor has it been widely appreciated, so the subject could not have been taught effectively in the past. Fortunately, things are changing now; the extensive illiteracy throughout English-speaking countries has excited much research. This adds authenticity to many small, enlightening experiments and discoveries currently being made by the few teachers who have the courage to probe. We are finding not only that it is pleasurable to teach reading and spelling by phonics, but also that hardly any pupils need to fail to learn to read.

I use these games in conjunction with Mrs Violet Brand's scheme, using the order in which the sounds are introduced in *SAM* (Egon). Each game supports and extends the new steps within the structure of the scheme, but they can be played in any order.

The games are unbelievably simple and, in principle, well within the capabilities of every potential reader. Significant progress is currently being realised by a ten-year-old boy who experienced boredom and failure; the games have revitalised his reading lessons. A girl aged eleven who spoke a dialect could not order the alphabet and despaired of ever learning to read. she now reads simple texts and plays the games with enjoyment.

Each game either practises and reinforces the sound/symbol relationship which has just been taught or introduces the pupil to the next one. Some games combine these two aims. When the games are presented to the pupil at the optimum moments in her reading development, newly learned rules are established. (NB We have used 'she' throughout this book to refer to the pupil. This is done purely for the purposes of consistency and clarity. It is not intended to imply that females have more problems with reading than males. In other books in the series we use 'he' throughout.)

Although these games can help any pupil to learn to read and spell, they have proved to be particularly useful and effective for pupils who have experienced years of failure in most of their school subjects because of their poor reading skills. One eight-year-old boy who was sent to me to receive 'help' draped himself over the back of his chair as we began the first lesson and refused to look at anything on the table. Learning to read had become anathema to him; he had received plenty of 'help', but he still couldn't read and so he had given up trying. His reaction presented a tense moment for me; I did not know him and I certainly did not want to spoil our relationship before it had even begun! I took out a game and shook the dice. 'Look Perry,' I said. 'I am playing a game, and I am winning.' Fortunately, he won … and gladly came again.

Success in winning the games does not depend on a pupil's ability to read or spell. The real secret of success lies in the fact that, quite subtly, the learning/teaching element is relegated to second place in favour of 'luck'. Because of this, pupils do not feel anxious when they play. There are no worries or tensions; they are confident that they **can** tackle something that appears to be so easy. In such a relaxed atmosphere, they can enjoy the fun of playing and even the triumph of beating the teacher! This latter achievement boosts the confidence of almost every pupil and it is very important to them. I have heard little ones discussing the play later in the day and looking very pleased with themselves as they've said, 'I won two games today.'

On the other hand, if the pupil loses, she can experience losing a game respectably, without any sense of failure, since she knows that she lost because the dice did not fall in her favour and definitely not because she was stupid!

Teachers will not, of course, be trying to win! On the contrary, and especially with younger pupils or those whose confidence needs to be built up, the teacher will contrive to lose the game! He or she will soon learn subtle ways to lose, by forgetting where the winning card is, by missing a turn, by always allowing the pupil to go first at the beginning of play, by working out whose will be the last card and by making helpful suggestions to the pupil so that she gets the advantage. I have also even turned a blind eye to a little cheating that works towards my purpose. Pupils have to know what they are doing in order to cheat … but of course I make it very clear that I do not approve of cheating and I correct it when I 'see' it!

Each game has its own very clear aim about which part of the reading structure it supports. There are, however, some subsidiary aims which make the games even more valuable; look out for these as you play.

ASSESSMENT

This is sometimes, for me, the main reason for playing a game. I often need to assess how much of the new work the pupil has assimilated and whether or not she is ready to go on. I assess the situation continually as I watch her strategies as she plays the game. I 'listen' to her thinking processes and to the use she makes of the sounds in the words. I need to know if she is really hearing the sounds or travelling down the dead-end road of remembering the words in 'look and say' fashion. If the latter is true, I know that more practice, more patient explanation and more adaptation to approach the problem from a different angle are all needed. During every game, I have to learn when to wait patiently for the pupil to remember and when to intervene with reassuring help. Playing these games has, in fact, helped me to be able to assess more precisely where my pupil is in her progress and how to help her move on.

VOCABULARY

Each of these games extends the pupils' spoken vocabulary as well as helping them to read and spell. I always talk to the pupils about the words we are using, about the meanings of the words and how they fit into sentences. I have been surprised by the number of pupils who do not know how to use some of the simple, three-letter words such as 'tub', 'wig', 'den' and 'pan', let alone the more difficult ones. I encourage the pupils to give clear definitions of the words to help them to remember when they later need to read them and use them in their own compositions.

MEMORY TRAINING

Memory training is intrinsic to many of the games and with some ingenuity on the part of the teacher even more use can be made of the games to help pupils remember than might at first be apparent. I often ask questions while we are playing, such as 'Where is the elephant?' or 'Is the stork under the "ar" or the "or"?' The most difficult part of learning to spell is remembering which symbol to use from the selection which represent the same sound: 'ai', 'ay', 'a-e' for example. Should 'rain' be spelled 'rane', 'rayne' or 'rain'? The games most certainly help to sort out problems of this kind.

As you become more familiar with the games, countless opportunities will occur to you to use the materials to test pupils' memory skills.

CONCLUSION

It has been my intention to make the games simple, attractive and fun to play. I have borne in mind, too, that they need to be played in a short time because I know from experience how little time many teachers have to spend with individual pupils.

I hope that the games can be photocopied cheaply so that copies may be taken home. Younger pupils especially like to share what they have enjoyed with their families and the additional practice will be good for them. Alternatively, sets of games can be made up and stored as a resource, which can be lent to parents and returned.

The clear aims and simple rules help parents to become effective teachers who, in turn, can give valuable help in playing the games with other pupils. The components of the games may also be used as a resource to illustrate specific teaching points. I have used the games in this way with older pupils who do not necessarily need the competitive approach.

The pictures will also inspire many useful worksheets and ideas for new games, so there are many uses for these photocopiable materials.

PLAYING THE GAMES

Most of the games are designed for two players who can either be the pupil and the teacher or two pupils playing together with the teacher or competent adult as referee. All reading games need supervision and mine are no exception, but the simplicity of these enables parents and classroom helpers to grasp the principles quickly to support the work of the teacher.

The rules of these games are very flexible and can be modified by the teacher to suit the pupil. Pupils sometimes change the rules and I have been happy to allow them to do that provided that the game is still fair and the main aims are accomplished.

There is a great deal of repetition of the rules across the selection of games. This aids the pupils' confidence and allows them to concentrate on the main purpose of the game without having to contend with more complicated instructions.

Pupils should move through the scheme at their own pace and teachers will find that there are more games for those sound/symbol groups that need most practice. Not all pupils need to play all of the games. Teachers need to be aware of an individual pupil's needs. There is little to be gained from playing a game once a pupil has understood that step, except, perhaps, to boost her confidence.

Teachers and helpers need to make sure that pupils know what the pictures represent before the game begins. Such a preview lends opportunity to talk about words and pictures and is an important part of the learning process.

HOW TO MAKE THE GAMES

○ Photocopy the required pages according to the instructions for each game, enlarging or reducing as you prefer. I made all my games to fit into zipped reading book folders measuring 40 x 27cm. This helps to keep the weight down when I have to carry a selection of games to school.

○ Colour the pictures; I have found coloured pencils to be the best tools to use. Enlist the help of anyone who is willing, but if you intend to make your games permanent, make sure that your 'colourers' have high standards.

○ Cut up the sheets as instructed and mount the pieces and the boards on card using an adhesive.

○ If you intend to cover your games with Tacky Back, (and this will certainly preserve them for much use in the future) then use water-based ink pens. Spirit-based ink spreads under Tacky Back. You may prefer to mount the games on thinner card and laminate them.

EXTRA EQUIPMENT REQUIRED

○ Nearly all of the games can be played in a shorter time, if necessary, so I find it useful to carry an egg-timer in my bag.

○ Blank dice can be obtained from:
Taskmaster Ltd, Morris Road, Leicester LE2 6BR

○ Make your feely bags from attractive pieces of material. Cut out a rectangle which is just a little longer than an A4 sheet of paper. Stitch the sides and hem the top. Thread a string through if you wish.

○ Buttons can be used for counters, or you can buy some from Taskmaster (see previous column). For 'counters' to move on the board, I collect trinkets or small toys from cereal packets. All these little novelties help to make the games more attractive.

○ Stock up with zipped reading book folders for simple storage. I label my folders with my own description of the contents so that I can find the game I need quickly. I also put a mounted copy of the rules for the game into the folder with the pieces.

○ Patience! – You will need much patience, too. If you have a will to teach reading, patience grows with the thrill of achievement in both pupil and teacher. I trust that these little games will bring much satisfaction to many people.

An emergency dice or spinner can be made using the pattern opposite. You can enlarge or reduce it according to your needs.

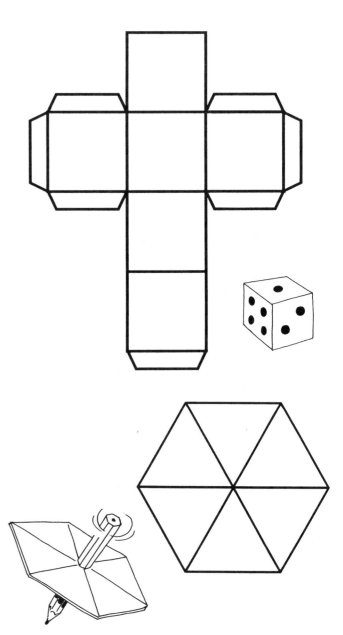

LEARNING TO RECOGNISE AND WRITE SOME OF THE PAIRS OF LETTERS THAT WORK TOGETHER TO SYMBOLISE A NEW SOUND

Using this Book

This digraphs book series covers the sounds 'ck', 'ee', 'oo', 'ar', 'or', 'sh', 'ch' and 'th'.

Before playing the games in this book, pupils will need to know that the twenty-six letters of the alphabet are symbols, or pictures of sounds. They should be able to recognise and translate those symbols into sounds and to 'hear' the sounds in simple words. They also should be able to write down the correct symbols for given sounds, independently. Extensive work will have been done on word building, enabling pupils to build three- or four-lettered words with sounds they know. They need to be able to read similar words by sounding out fairly competently.

As pupils approach this new stage in their learning, they will need to know that some sounds have to be represented by two or more letters working together. I explain that 26 letters are not enough to represent all the 44 sounds that come out of our mouths when we speak, so we need to make more 'pictures'. I demonstrate this by asking if one letter will represent the sound 'ch' or I say, 'Can you find a letter that will stand for "ar" in the word "park"?' These new pictures are not of letters **blending** together, as 'bl', 'cr', 'nd', 'fl' and many others do, but together they represent a brand new sound.

It is at this stage that teachers may want to consider the validity of the 'onset and rime' method of teaching phonics. As a part of this scheme, pupils are expected to learn a whole range of blends as if they are pictures of sounds.

In my experience, I have found there to be quite enough symbols for **new** sounds to be learned without confusing pupils by expecting them to **learn** the blends as if they were all sound symbols. Indeed, I have met pupils whose progress has been seriously hindered by well-meaning teachers who have burdened the pupils by trying to teach them all the blends. The secret lies in **hearing** the **separate sounds**, then gradually with experience, learning to recognise and blend them speedily.

Pupils will need careful tuition before tackling each new sound symbol. I show them how the letters in a blend keep their own sounds, but letters that work together have to change. We listen to 'o' for 'orange' and 'o' for 'ostrich', then we put the two 'o's together to make 'oo'. We then look at some words which have 'oo' and we notice the difference between the 'oo' in 'look' and the sound of 'oo' in 'room'. Saying the words and writing them all helps to fix them in the pupils' memory.

I do not usually worry the pupils with rules at this stage; they have quite enough to cope with, but teachers who take the trouble to investigate will find that the rules that govern phonics are extremely interesting, fascinating and useful.

Find the Beginning
('ck' words)

AIM

○ To familiarise the pupils with the sound and symbol 'ck' in one-syllable words.

HOW TO MAKE THE GAME

○ Cut up the cards that show the vowel, 'ck' and picture. Cut off the initial sound as indicated.

HOW TO PLAY

○ Arrange the initial sounds neatly, face down on the table.

○ Deal three picture cards to each player.

○ Players take turns to select an initial sound card. If they can complete one of their words with it, they may keep the pair and put it to one side. They then take another picture card to replace it.

○ When all the cards have been used up, the winner is the player who has the most completed words.

TEACHER GUIDANCE

FIND THE BEGINNING AND FIND THE ENDING

'ck' is, surprisingly, one of the most difficult sound symbols for young or inexperienced spellers to use in their work. Once they have learned to put 'c' and 'k' together, they want to write the symbol every time they hear the 'k' sound in a word. They need to learn that if a single syllable word needs a 'short' vowel sound and ends with a 'k' sound, then they need to put 'ck', as in 'sack', 'peck', 'pick', 'sock' and 'duck'. I explain to them, 'If you cannot hear the short vowel sound (I demonstrate what I mean by 'short'; pupils will probably not know what you mean by the word but it is useful for them to know) as in such words as "dark", "park", "cake", "look", "bike" and so on, then put a "k" on its own.'

When I am dictating to pupils, I emphasise the 'ck' ending by asking them, 'How do you write that good, strong "k" sound when it comes after "a", "e", "i", "o", "u"?' (I say the sounds not the letter names.)

Strictly speaking 'ck' is not a digraph. It is used when a double 'k' sound is required. The games that introduce 'ck' do, however, seem to be best placed in this book.

r ock	l ock	cr ack	s ack	cl ock

ick	**ock**	**ock**	**uck**	**ack**
k	**s**	**fl**	**d**	**bl**

br icks	n eck	l ick	st ick	p ick

Find the Ending
('ck' words)

AIM

○ To give continued practice in hearing the 'ck' sound and reading and spelling 'ck' words.

HOW TO MAKE THE GAME

○ Cut up the sheets to make cards and cut off the picture and initial sound as indicated. Cut up the sheet of 'yes' and 'no' cards and place them in a feely bag. (The 'yes' and 'no' cards may be photocopied twice and the words stuck back to back so that the cards are double-sided.)

WHAT YOU NEED

○ A feely bag.

HOW TO PLAY

○ Sort out the vowel plus 'ck' cards. Place them on the table so that sounds of a kind are together, with letters upmost.

○ Stack the picture with initial sound cards and then deal three of these cards to each player.

○ Players should place their three picture cards in front of them on the table.

○ Players then draw from the feely bag. If a 'yes' card is drawn, that player may match one of her pictures with a vowel plus 'ck' card and set the word aside. She may then take another picture card. If a 'no' card is drawn that player misses a turn.

○ The game ends when all the cards have been used up. The winner is the player with the most completed words.

SOME 'CK' WORDS TO READ AND SPELL

pick	black
sack	clock
lick	flock
suck	brick
duck	crack
lock	stick
sock	
neck	
rock	
back	
kick	

r ock	l ock	s ock	d uck	p ick

ack	ack	ock	ock	ack
s	cr	cl	fl	bl

st	s	k	br	c
ick	uck	ick	icks	ock

yes	yes	yes	yes	no	no
yes	yes	yes	yes	no	no
yes	yes	yes	yes	no	no
yes	yes	yes	yes	no	no

Give the Dog a Bone
(single-syllable 'ck' words)

AIMS

○ To practise using the sound 'ck' with all five vowel sounds in single-syllable words.

○ To expand the pupils' vocabulary as well as extending the numbers of words they can read and spell.

HOW TO MAKE THE GAME

○ Photocopy the sheets of dogs and bones (pages 18 and 24) so that you have 24 dog cards and 24 bone cards in all (you will need to discard three dogs). Photocopy the word cards (page 19 to 23). Cut up all the cards – dogs, words and bones. Stick half of the word cards onto the backs of the dog cards and the other half onto the backs of the bone cards so that the cards can be paired by their vowel sound (for example, 'brick' on a bone card and 'pick' on a dog card).

HOW TO PLAY

○ Scatter the bone cards, bone side up, over the table. Deal three dog cards to each player, who should place the cards, word side up in front of her on the table. The rest of the dog cards should be stacked.

○ The players take turns to select a bone card. If the card pairs with any of their dog cards, they may keep the pair, set it aside and take another dog card from the stack. If the bone card cannot be paired, it must be returned to the table and the next player has her turn. If she has been watching carefully, she will know whether or not she needs the bone to pair with one of her cards.

○ The game continues until all the cards are paired. The winner is the player with the most pairs.

TEACHER GUIDANCE

All these 'ck' games should help establish the proper use of 'ck', especially if the teacher bears in mind the rule and endeavours to pass it on to the pupil in digestible form.

As we are playing this game, I draw attention to the 'ack', 'eck', 'ick', 'ock' and 'uck' parts of the words. I stop occasionally to ask, 'How would you use this word when you are speaking?' I choose those words I think the pupil may not have met before, thus making an opportunity to enlarge her vocabulary. We always have an interesting discussion about the word 'wreck' – in my game, the silent 'w' is emphasised in red ink. I tell the pupil about 'wrong' and 'write' (and right!) not expecting her to remember how to spell these words at this stage, but to illustrate, as I often do, the endless fascination of words.

truck	mock	luck
suck	lick	kick
nick	back	lock

peck	rock	flock
tick	muck	prick
pick	pack	brick

wick	trick	sack
Jack	neck	rack
snack	stuck	black

pluck	sick	tuck
deck	block	click
crack	duck	sock

tack	stick	Mick
quack	smack	wreck
slack	check	clock

speck	frock	flick

Missing 'oo's and 'ee's

AIM

○ To practise or prepare for the sounds represented by 'oo' and 'ee' in words.

HOW TO MAKE THE GAME

○ Cut up the sheets of pictures with their incomplete words to make them into individual cards. Make small 'oo and 'ee' cards by cutting up the sheet of these sounds and trimming them so that they fit between the consonants (page 30). I usually make a few more than I require.

WHAT YOU NEED

○ A feely bag for the 'oo' and 'ee' cards.

HOW TO PLAY

○ Shuffle the picture/word cards and deal three cards to each player. Stack the rest.

○ Players take turns to take one small card from the feely bag. If one of their three words can be completed with the 'oo' or 'ee' drawn, they may set the card aside and take another from the stack. If they cannot use the small card, it should be returned to the bag.

○ The game continues until all the picture/word cards have been used up. The winner is the player with the most completed word cards.

TEACHER GUIDANCE

THE 'OO'/'EE' GAMES: MISSING 'OO'S AND 'EE'S AND THE 'OO'/'EE' GAME

Before play begins, study the pictures and make sure that the pupil can hear the oo/ee sounds in the word for each one. I never take it for granted that the pupils know what the pictures represent and am ever watchful for the one who returns her 'oo'/'ee' card to the bag when she does need it. This may be because she has not linked the right word with the picture, thinking that 'see' is 'look', for instance, or 'street' is 'road'.
I talk about the word 'meet' with the pupil and explain that this is the word we use when mum or dad comes to get them from school, and it has nothing to do with the meat that we eat.

We listen to the difference between the 'oo' sound in 'roof' and in 'foot'. We listen to the rhyme of 'boot' and 'root' but we can hear that 'foot' will not join in (except in some dialects).

I try to introduce a little advice about other words as we play. 'See' and 'bee' will rhyme with 'tree' but 'be' doesn't buzz. We think of sentences in which these words could be used. 'Sweet', 'meet' and 'feet' all rhyme with 'street' but 'str' has three consonants strung together and the pupils need to be helped to hear all of them. I show them what happens if we leave one of those consonants out of the word.

I help the pupils to say the word 'stool' properly. I tell them that our tongues are lazy when the letter 'l' comes at or near the end of the word. I find it useful to have a small mirror handy so that they can see the position of the tongue, teeth and lips when they say the sound 'l'. Some young pupils know what a cotton reel is for but the word 'reel' needs explanation. An understanding of correct speech is essential for correct spelling.

l	t	d	t	p
st	b	f	r	sl

b

t
f

p
p

p
sw

l
r

s	t	t	tr	m
	str	sw		t

f	m	n	n	t
r	br	sp	m	f

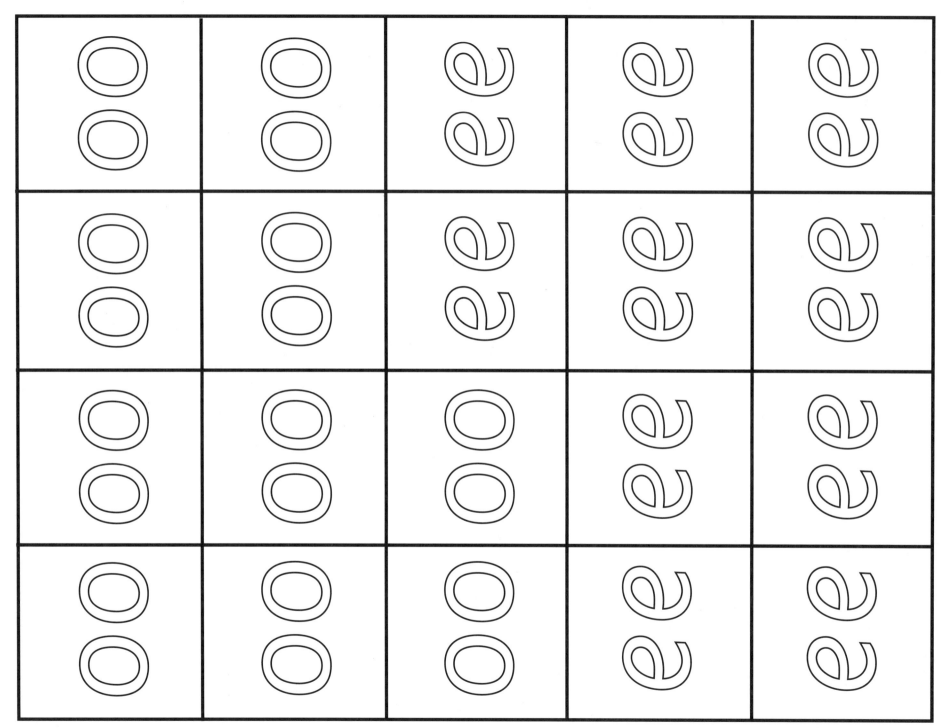

The 'oo/ee' Matching Game

AIM

○ To practise words containing the 'oo' or the 'ee' sound.

HOW TO MAKE THE GAME

○ The four sheets of picture/word cards are in two pairs (pages 32 and 33; pages 34 and 35). One of each pair has the word and the other has the picture to go with it. For each pair, cut up one of the sheets into small cards. The remaining sheet is the board. Write 'w' on the reverse of each word card and 'p' on the reverse of each picture card.

WHAT YOU NEED

○ A dice with two sides marked with a 'w', two sides marked with a 'p', one side marked with a red spot and the remaining side marked with an orange spot.

○ A shaking cup.

HOW TO PLAY

○ Make two stacks, one with the 'p' cards and the other with the 'w' cards, picture or word side down.

○ Players take turns to throw the dice. If the 'w' is thrown, the player may take a 'w' card and match it, if she can, with a picture on her board. If she cannot match it, it should be returned to the stack and 'buried'. The same procedure applies for a 'p' card. If a red spot is thrown, the player misses a turn, but if an orange spot is thrown, the player may choose to take a 'p' or 'w' card.

○ The winner is the player who fills her board first.

TEACHER GUIDANCE

I have learned that a little sleight of hand helps this game along. If the pupil selects a card that I need, I encourage him to tuck it back in the pile. If I select a card that my pupil needs, I leave it on the top. Even my older pupils appear to be unaware of this little trick – or maybe they do notice and make use of my naivety.

Make sure that each pupil is naming the pictures correctly. Check this by asking 'What word will you need for this picture?' and 'Which picture will go with this word?'.

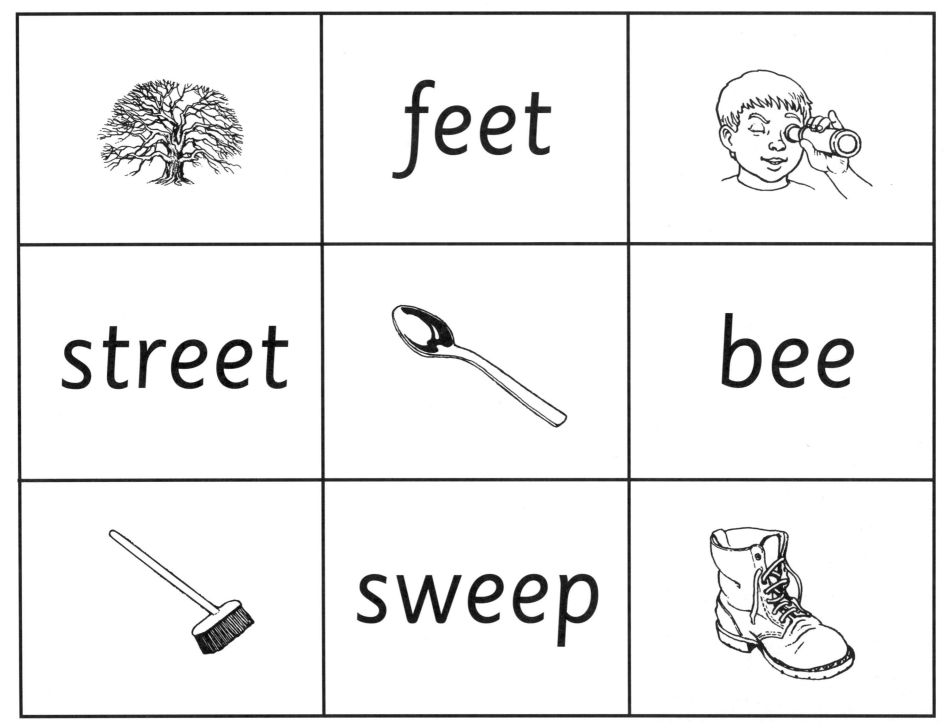

tree | feet | (boy with telescope)

street | (spoon) | bee

(brush) | sweep | (boot)

tree	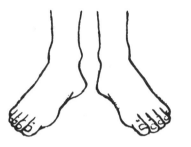	see
	spoon	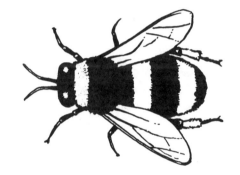
broom		boot

	sleep	
meet		roof
	food	

stool		moon
	peep	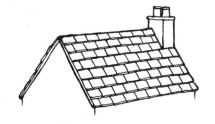
foot		sweet

The 'ar'/'or' Game

AIMS

❍ To practise hearing and comparing the 'ar' and 'or' sounds in words.

❍ To practise spelling the words.

HOW TO MAKE THE GAME

❍ There are two boards (pages 37 and 38) – one has six 'or' sounds and the other has six 'ar' sounds. The picture sheets (pages 39 and 40) should be cut up to make small cards. The word for each picture(pages 41 and 42) should be pasted to the reverse of each card.

WHAT YOU NEED

❍ A dice on which the sound symbol 'ar' has been marked on three sides and 'or' marked on the remaining three sides.

❍ A shaking cup.

HOW TO PLAY

❍ Scatter the cards, picture side up, over the table.

❍ Each player has a board and must collect pictures with words containing the sound written on her board.

❍ Players take turns to throw the dice. If the player with the 'ar' board throws 'ar' on the dice, she may select a picture of a word containing the 'ar' sound, check the back of the card to make sure she is correct, read the word and place the card on her board. If 'or' is thrown, then that player cannot move yet.

❍ The first player to fill her board is the winner. I exercise leniency according to the ability of the pupil. A wrong choice of picture, followed by some advice and the opportunity to have another 'go', helps towards success.

TEACHER GUIDANCE

THE 'AR'/'OR' GAME AND THE 'AR'/'OR' QUICKIE

Before beginning to play these games, make sure the pupil knows what the pictures represent. She may not know what a harp is, or a barn, or a stork, and may not recognise the tart or the storm. I talk to the pupils about these things. Each of them presents a wonderful opportunity for a profitable conversation.
'What kind of tart do you like best? In our house, we like treacle tart. What else can you put into a tart?'
I tell the pupils what I know about the stork. It is known to many as the bird on the margarine packet.
I sometimes show them the wrapping paper with the 'or' sound symbol in the word.

As we play, the youngest pupils soon discover that, if I reject a card because I have no picture for it on the board, then it must be one they need and they snatch it up with glee and win! To retain an element of suspense for older pupils, I reshuffle the cards each time an unwanted one is replaced.

'or' is one of the sound pictures that many pupils find difficult to memorise whilst 'ar' seems to be among the easiest to remember. I do not know why that should be but I bear it in mind when we are playing and I emphasise the 'or' words more carefully. I help the pupil to feel the sound in her mouth when she says the words, and we compare the sounds in 'fork' and 'walk', sometimes using a mirror to see the position of lips, tongue and teeth when these words are spoken.

or	or	or
or	or	or

ar	ar	ar
ar	ar	ar

horse	stork	porch
storm	fork	torch
cork	torn	corn

barn	harp	arm
dart	tart	scarf
car	jar	shark

The 'ar'/'or' Quickie

AIMS

○ To help pupils to hear the 'ar' and 'or' sounds in words.

○ To practise listening for the correct sound.

HOW TO MAKE THE GAME

The picture cards (pages 44 and 45) are the boards. Cut up the sheet of 'ar' and 'or' symbols (page 46) to make them into small cards.

HOW TO PLAY

○ Each player chooses a board. Shuffle the small cards and place them in neat rows on the table, letter side down.

○ Players take turns to select a small card. This is then placed appropriately, if possible, on their board.

○ The first player to cover all her pictures with symbols is the winner.

MORE IDEAS FOR PLAYING

○ You need one copy each of the picture cards (pages 44 and 45) and two copies each of the letter cards (page 46). Scatter all the cards over the table, the picture cards picture side up and the word cards face down. Let the pupil choose a picture then turn over a letter card to see if a pair can be made. If not, she must wait for her next turn to try again. The winner collects the most pairs in a given time, or when all the picture cards have been used up.

○ Photocopy the picture cards once and the letter cards twice. Each player chooses nine picture cards and arranges them neatly, picture side up on the table. The letter cards are stacked in two piles, one for 'ar' and one for 'or'. Players take turns to throw the 'ar'/'or' dice (see page 36) and match one of their pictures with its letter card as appropriate. The winner is the first player to pair all of her pictures with sound cards.

TEACHER GUIDANCE

I try to make a point of telling my pupils what we are doing and why we are doing it. Even the little ones try to understand. We are not just playing games for fun, although we do enjoy playing them. Really, we are helping our minds to remember the sounds as they look when they are written down. Sometimes I say 'When you see this letter, (I write an 'a') you know immediately that it stands for 'a' (I say the sound). I want you to be able to look at 'or' and 'ar' and to know, just as quickly, what those letters stand for.

44

or	or	or	or
or	or	ar	ar
ar	ar	ar	ar

The 'sh'/'ch' Games

AIM

○ To practise listening for and preparing to meet the 'sh' and 'ch' sound symbols in words.

GAME 1: PICTURE MATCH

HOW TO MAKE THE GAME

○ The picture cards (pages 49 and 50) are the boards. Cut up the sheet of 'sh' and 'ch' symbols (pages 51 and 52) to make them into small cards.

WHAT YOU NEED

○ A dice with 'sh' marked on three sides and 'ch' marked on the remaining three sides.

○ A shaking cup.

HOW TO PLAY

○ Each player has a board and the 'sh'/'ch' cards are placed centrally on the table with the letters facing up.

○ Players take turns to throw the dice and take a small card from the pool to match what was thrown. If one of the pictures on the player's board has that sound in its word, the picture may be covered with the small card. If the player cannot use the card, it is returned to the pool.

○ The game continues until one player, the winner, has covered all her pictures with cards.

○ Alternatively, the teacher may discuss the sounds and pictures with the pupil first, and place the small cards on the appropriate pictures. The game can then be played in reverse, and the winner is the first player to empty her board.

GAME 2: FIRST TO SIX (A VARIATION OF GAME 1)

HOW TO MAKE THE GAME

○ Cut up both the pictures and the sounds. Make the picture into small cards and affix the sh/ch symbols appropriately to the reverse of each card.

WHAT YOU NEED

○ A dice marked with 'sh' on three sides and with 'ch' on the remaining three sides.

○ A shaking cup.

HOW TO PLAY

○ All the cards should be placed neatly on the table, picture side up.

○ Players take turns to throw the dice. Each player must try to collect six pictures illustrating the same sound. The sounds collected may be mutually agreed, or decided by the player's first throw. The winner is the first player to collect six pictures illustrating her 'sound'.

CONTINUED FROM PAGE 47

The 'sh'/'ch' Games

TEACHER GUIDANCE

Before play begins, check that the pupil knows what each picture represents and that she can hear the 'sh' or 'ch' sound when it comes at the beginning or the end of a word.

Use every opportunity to discuss the sounds in the words but do not worry the pupil at this stage with the spellings of the words with sound pictures which you have not dealt with in your structured phonics lessons. When I play this game with the pupils, I know that they are able, with their new knowledge of 'sh' and 'ch', to sound out and spell 'chin', 'ship', 'shop', 'shed', 'shell', 'chicks', 'fish', 'dish', 'rash', 'brush' and 'splash'. I help them to hear the 'n' in 'lunch' and 'bench' and we consider what would happen if we left the 'n' out. I help them to **hear** that 'beach' and 'peach' are alike and ask questions such as, 'How are they alike? What word would be left if we took away the "b" or the "p"?'

Knowing that, in the programme I use, the pupil will soon be meeting the sounds in ch**ai**n and sh**ir**t, I draw attention to these **sounds** without showing the written symbols at this stage.

For the last seven words – 'shoe', 'chocolate', 'patch', 'match', 'switch', 'cherries' and 'chair' – I only require the pupil to hear the 'sh' or 'ch' sound, but teachers will know the ability of their pupils and some will be able to explain the phonic patterns in these words to enable the pupil to spell them.

WORDS USED IN THESE GAMES

beach	fish
match	dish
bench	brush
lunch	rash
peach	splash
patch	ship
switch	shoe
chin	shop
cherry	shed
chocolate	shell
chair	shirt
chain	
chicks	

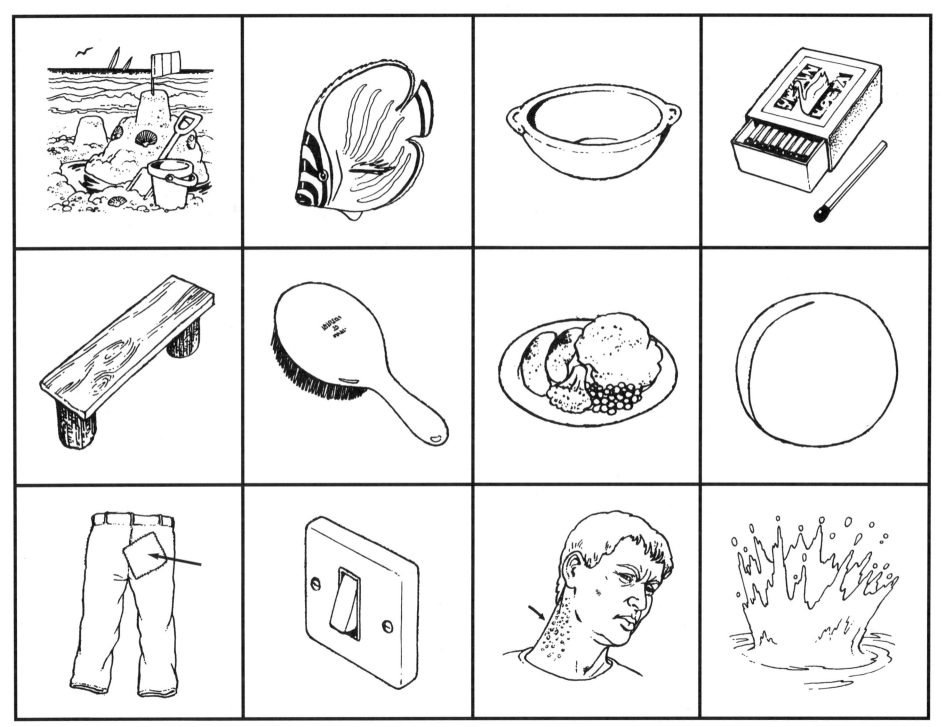

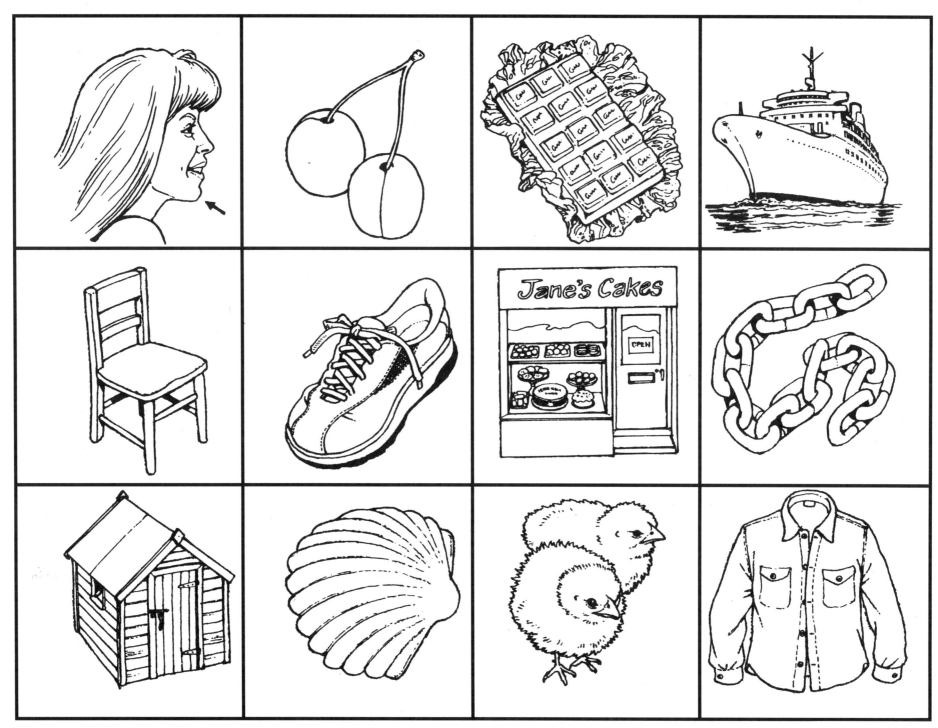

ch	sh	sh	ch
ch	sh	ch	ch
ch	ch	sh	sh

ch	ch	ch	sh
ch	sh	sh	ch
sh	sh	ch	sh

The Tongue-Between-Your-Teeth Game

AIM

○ To practise saying and using the sound represented by the symbol 'th'.

HOW TO MAKE THE GAME

○ Cut along all the lines on the two sheets (pages 54 and 55) so that you have 15 long cards showing incomplete words, and 27 small cards, which are mainly 'th' cards but six have 'sh' and six have 'ch'. Colour the outlined letters.

WHAT YOU NEED

○ A feely bag large enough to contain the 27 small cards.

HOW TO PLAY

○ Set out the 15 incomplete words on the table so that they are all visible.

○ Shuffle the small cards in the feely bag.

○ Players take turns to dip into the bag and draw out a small card. If it has 'th' on it, that player may use it to complete one of the words set out on the table. The player may choose which word she completes, but she must read the completed word. If it is read correctly, she may keep the card.

○ If a 'ch' or a 'sh' card is drawn, it cannot be used to make a word, even if the pairing is possible (chin, for example) – only 'th' words are valid. Such a card is not replaced in the feely bag, but is set aside out of the game, and the player misses the turn.

○ When the word cards are all used up, the player with the most completed words is the winner.

TEACHER GUIDANCE

Pupils soon learn to read the sound symbol 'th' and put their tongue between their teeth readily enough when they meet a 'th' word in their books, but they are often confused about when to say 'th' in their speech or when to write it in their spelling.

Pupils often look at me when I am dictating sentences for them to write; they need a clue when they are not sure whether to write 'th', 'f' or 'v'. I find this game very useful in helping to establish which words have the 'th' sound in them. I use my small mirrors to show the pupils where their tongues should be when they say these words.

If you listen to pupils talking, you will hear that the sound 'th' is much under used. They speak of 'muvver', 'farver', 'dis' and 'dat' and confuse the words 'free' and 'three'. I tell the pupils that they may speak as they wish in the playground but in my lesson, in order to hear the correct sounds, they must speak 'posh'. I use these games to help sort out speech problems as well as to establish the sound symbol 'th' in their memories.

mo	th	sh	th	ick
fro	th	sh	th	at
clo	th	sh	th	em
wi	th	sh	th	ing

th	ump	th	ank	ch
th	is	th	ree	ch
th	en	th	ink	ch
th	in	sh	sh	ch	ch	ch

The 'sh'/'ch'/'th' Game

AIMS

○ To give experience in selecting the correct symbol when hearing 'sh', 'ch' or 'th' at the beginning or end of a word.

HOW TO MAKE THE GAME

○ Cut along all the lines on the sheets on pages 57 to 61 so that you have 24 picture cards, 12 incomplete 'th' word cards and 24 incomplete 'sh' and 'ch' word cards. Stick each incomplete word card on the reverse of its picture so that, for example, 'ips' will be on the back of the picture of a plate of chips. The 'th' words (page 59) have no pictures. Also cut up the page of 'th', 'sh' and 'ch' sounds (page 62) to make small cards. You may want to colour these in. I use red ink for 'th', green for 'sh' and blue for 'ch'.

WHAT YOU NEED

○ A bag in which to store the 36 small 'th'/'sh'/'ch' cards.

○ A dice marked with 'th' on two sides, 'sh' on two sides and 'ch' on the remaining two sides.

○ A shaking cup.

HOW TO PLAY

○ Scatter the 'th'/'sh'/'ch' small cards on the table. The colours will help to make the symbols more easily visible.

○ Shuffle the incomplete word/picture cards and deal nine cards to each player. Players should then place these cards in front of them, so that all the cards can be seen, picture side up (except the 'th' cards, which must be word side up.)

○ Players take turns to throw the dice. If 'th' is thrown (for example), the player must take a 'th' card from the pool and use it to complete one of her words. She misses a go if she has no card that needs a 'th'.

○ The winner is the player who completes all of her nine words first.

○ The number of cards dealt to the players is at the teacher's discretion. If you are short of time, deal six. If you wish, you may lengthen the game by dealing out all of the cards.

TEACHER GUIDANCE

All of the pictures in this game illustrate words that contain the symbols 'sh' or 'ch'. Some discussion will be required, prior to play, to help the pupil understand that the sound 'ch' is not in 'trousers' but is in 'patch'; that the picture featuring a sandcastle illustrates the word 'beach'; that the arrow is pointing to 'chin' which is part of 'face' and that the picture of food is illustrating the word 'lunch'. The rash on the man's neck will need some explanation, too, and the difference between 'seat' and 'bench' needs to be pointed out.

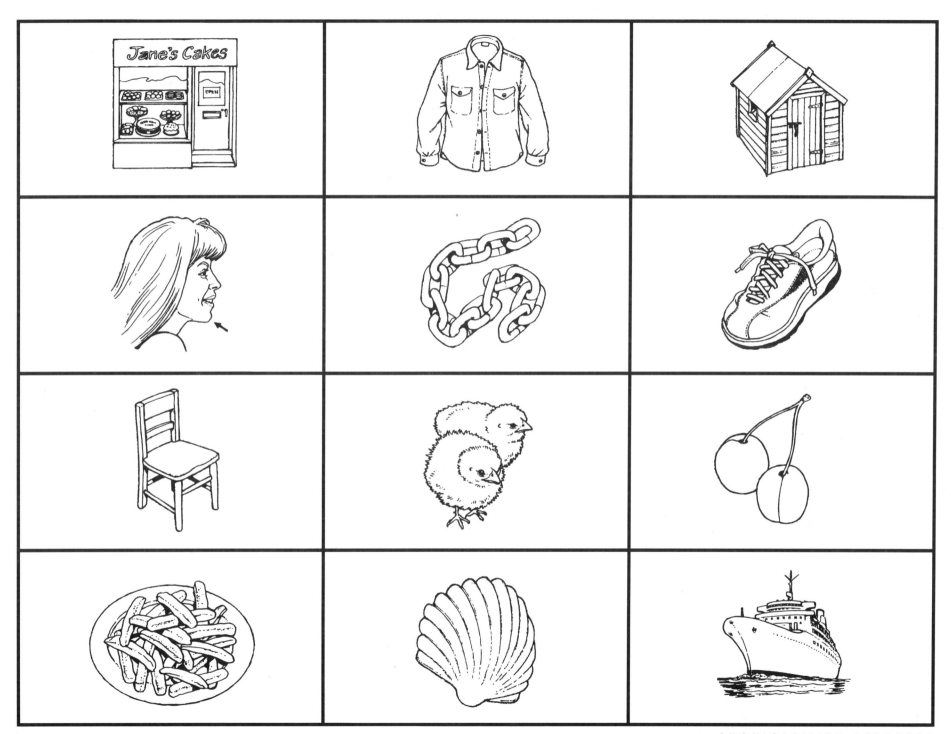

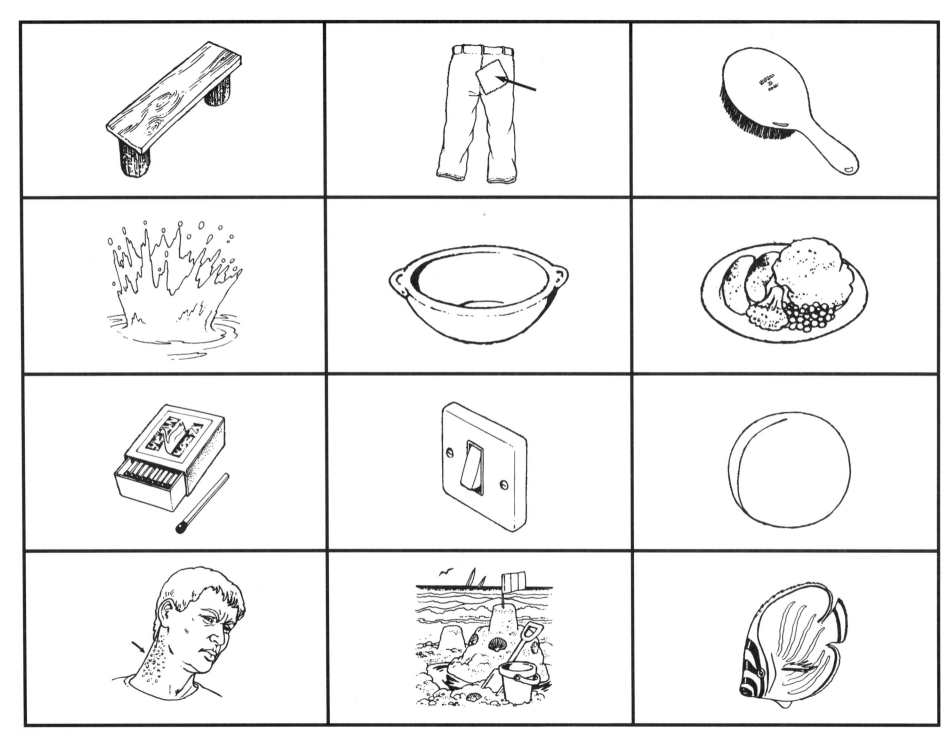

at	ink	ank
is	ick	mo
en	ree	clo
in	em	wi

ben	pat	bru
spla	di	lun
mat	swit	pea
ra	bea	fi

op	irt	ed
in	ain	oe
air	icks	erries
ips	ell	ip

th	th	th	sh	sh	sh	ch	ch	ch
th	th	th	sh	sh	sh	ch	ch	ch
th	th	th	sh	sh	sh	ch	ch	ch
th	th	th	sh	sh	sh	ch	ch	ch